VIOLIN TUNES
MADE EASY
by William Bay

MB22110
LARGE PRINT
BIG NOTE
EDITION

Visit us on the Web at www.melbay.com or billsmusicshelf.com

Table of Contents

Haul Away, Joe 3
Green Grow the Lilacs 4
Tenting Tonight.............5
Aloha Oe 6
Lament 7
The Foggy, Foggy Dew 8
The Ash Grove.............9
One More River.............10
Auld Lang Syne 11
Strawberry Roan 12
Johnny Has Gone for a Soldier 14
Ol' Dan Tucker 15
Blow Away the Morning Dew.............16
Bell Bottom Trousers.............17
Old Shoe Boots & Leggins 18
Wait Til the Sun Shines Nellie 19
At a Georgia Camp Meeting 20
Marchin' to Glory 21
Goin' South 22
Oh, Sinner Man 23
Come & Go with Me to that Land 24
Bile' Dem Cabbage Down 25
Goober Peas.............26
Captain Kidd 27
The Fish of the Sea 28
Jolly Old Roger 29
My Bonnie 30
The Bold Fisherman 31
High Barbaree 32
Greenland Fishery 33
Blow, Ye Winds 34
Cripple Creek.............35
Sourwood Mountain 36
Big Rock Candy Mountain 37
The Roving Cowboy 38
When Jesus Wept.............39
Blessed Quietness 40
There's a River of Life 41
When I Can Read My Title Clear 42
Praise the Savior 43
Great God When I Approach Thy Throne.............44
Must Jesus Bear the Cross Alone 45
I am Bound for the Promised Land.............46
When Jesus Left His Father's Throne 47
Jesus Calls Us 48
Lonesome Valley 49

The Galway Races.............50
Cockles & Mussels 51
The Wild Rover 52
Love is Teasin' 53
The Galway Shawl 54
The Rose of Tralee 55
Brian O'Linn 56
Spancil Hill 57
Si Beag Si Mór 58
Bunclody 59
My Mary of the Curling Hair 60
Musetta's Waltz 61
Drink to Me Only with Thine Eyes.............62
Southern Roses 63
Gypsy Theme 64
Hatikvoh 65
Santa Lucia 66
Tis So Sweet 67
I Need Thee Every Hour 68
Precious Memories 69
Mandy Lee.............70
Daisy Bell 71
Up in a Balloon 72
Strike Up the Band 73
This Little Light of Mine.............74
Silver Threads Among the Gold 75
Grandfather's Clock 76
All God's Children Got Shoes.............77
Little David Play on Your Harp.............78
If You're Happy and You Know It 79
I've Got Peace Like a River 80
Bringing In the Sheaves 81
In the Pines 82
The Battle Cry of Freedom 83
Nine Hundred Miles 84
Down Where the Cotton Blossoms Grow 85
America the Beautiful 86
Our Boys Will Shine Tonight 87
Columbia, the Gem of the Ocean 88
Mama Don't 'Low 90
She'll be Comin' Round the Mountain 91
Loch Lomond 92
Crawdad Song 93
The Mermaid 94
The Old Oaken Bucket 95
Doxology 96

Haul Away, Joe

Green Grow the Lilacs

Tenting Tonight

Aloha Oe

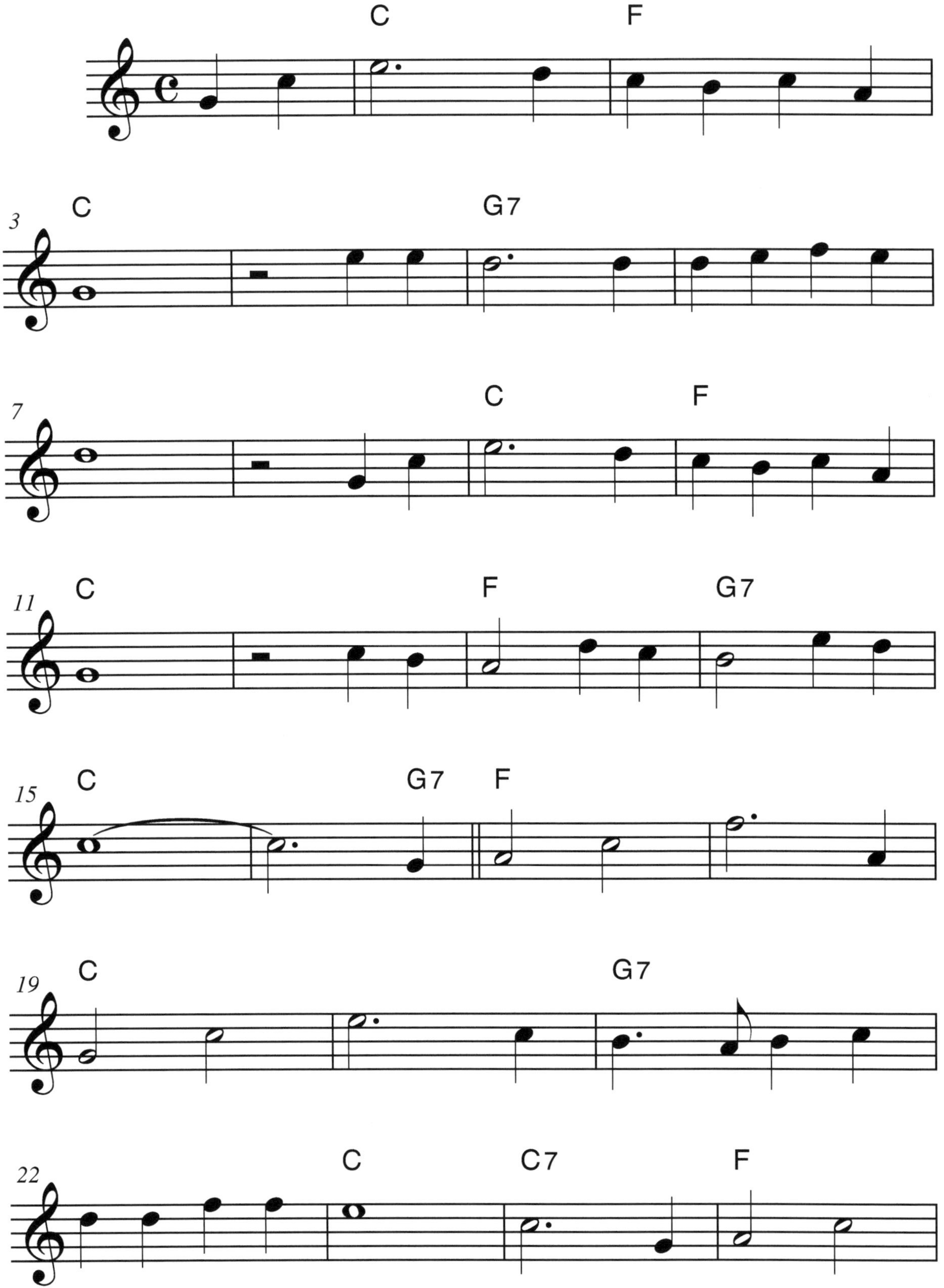

C
F
C
G7
C
F
C
F
G7
C
G7
F
C
G7
C
C7
F

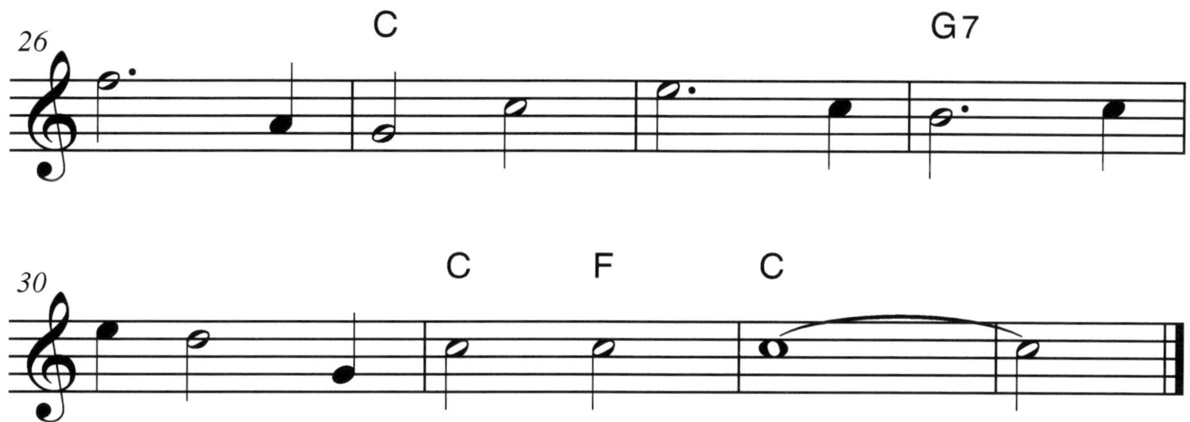
26
C
G7
30
C F C

Lament

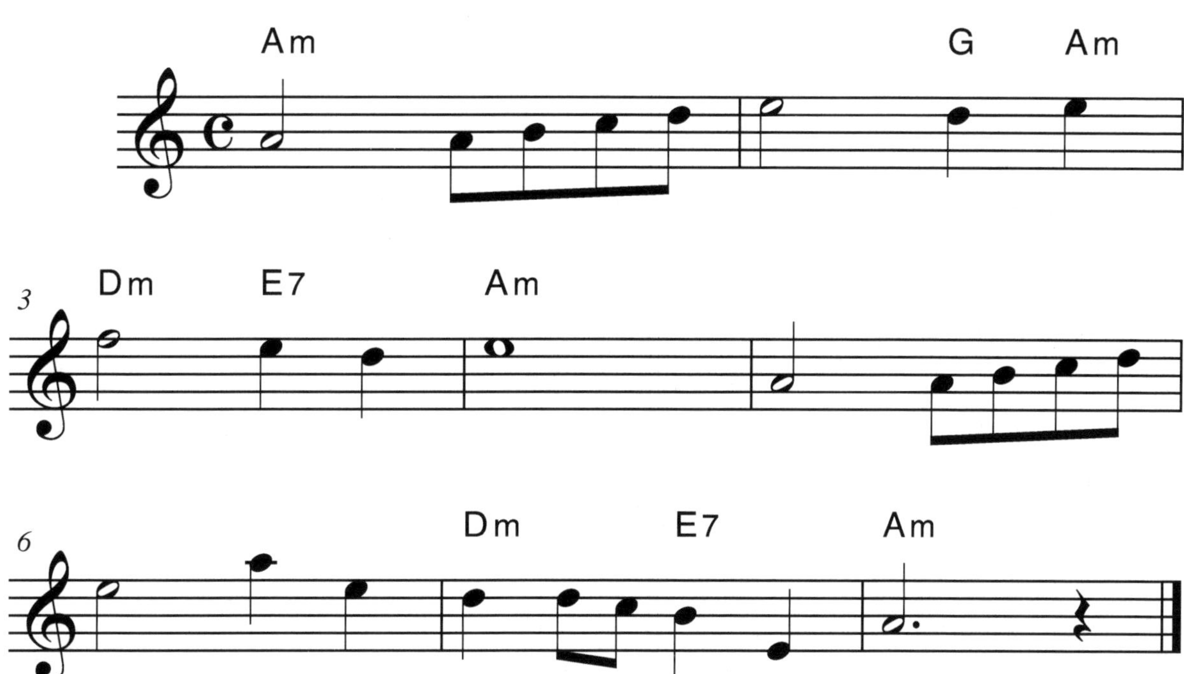
Am
G Am
Dm E7 Am
3
6
Dm E7 Am

The Foggy, Foggy Dew

The Ash Grove

One More River

Auld Lang Syne

Strawberry Roan

F
G7
C
F
G7
C
F
C
F
C
F
C
G7
C

Johnny Has Gone for a Soldier

Ol' Dan Tucker

Blow Away the Morning Dew

Bell Bottom Trousers

Old Shoe Boots & Leggins

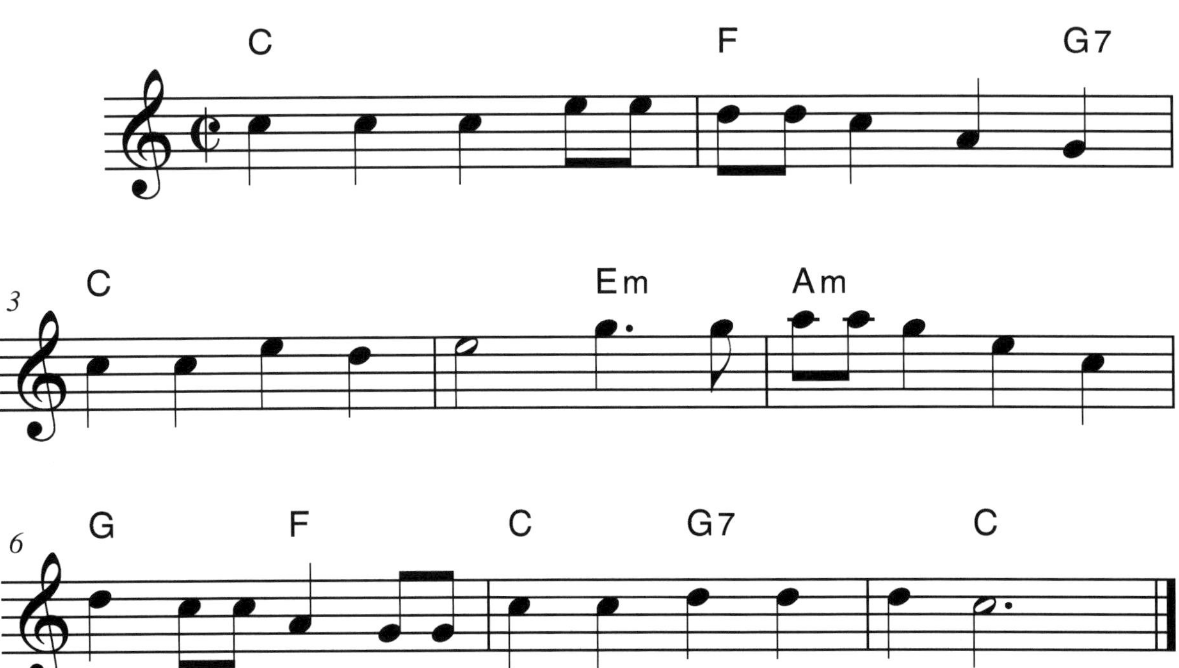

Wait Till the Sun Shines Nellie

At a Georgia Camp Meeting

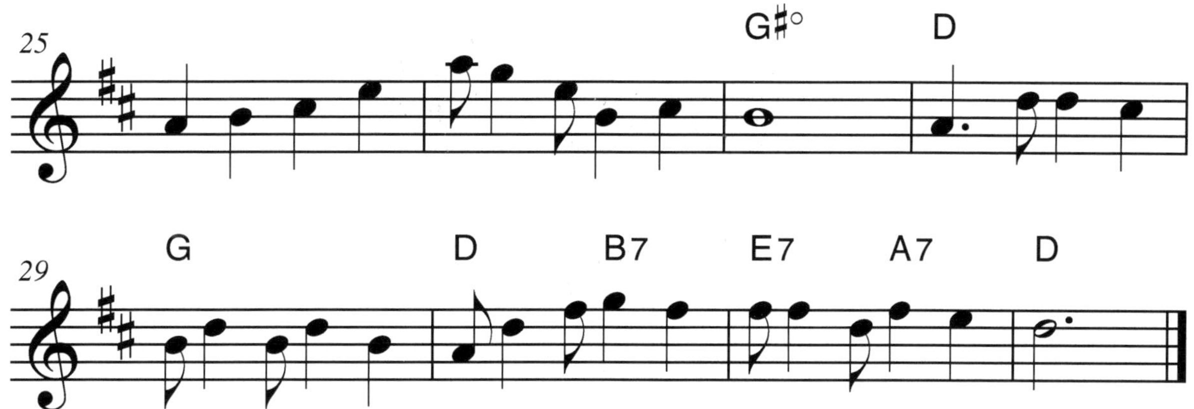

Marchin' to Glory

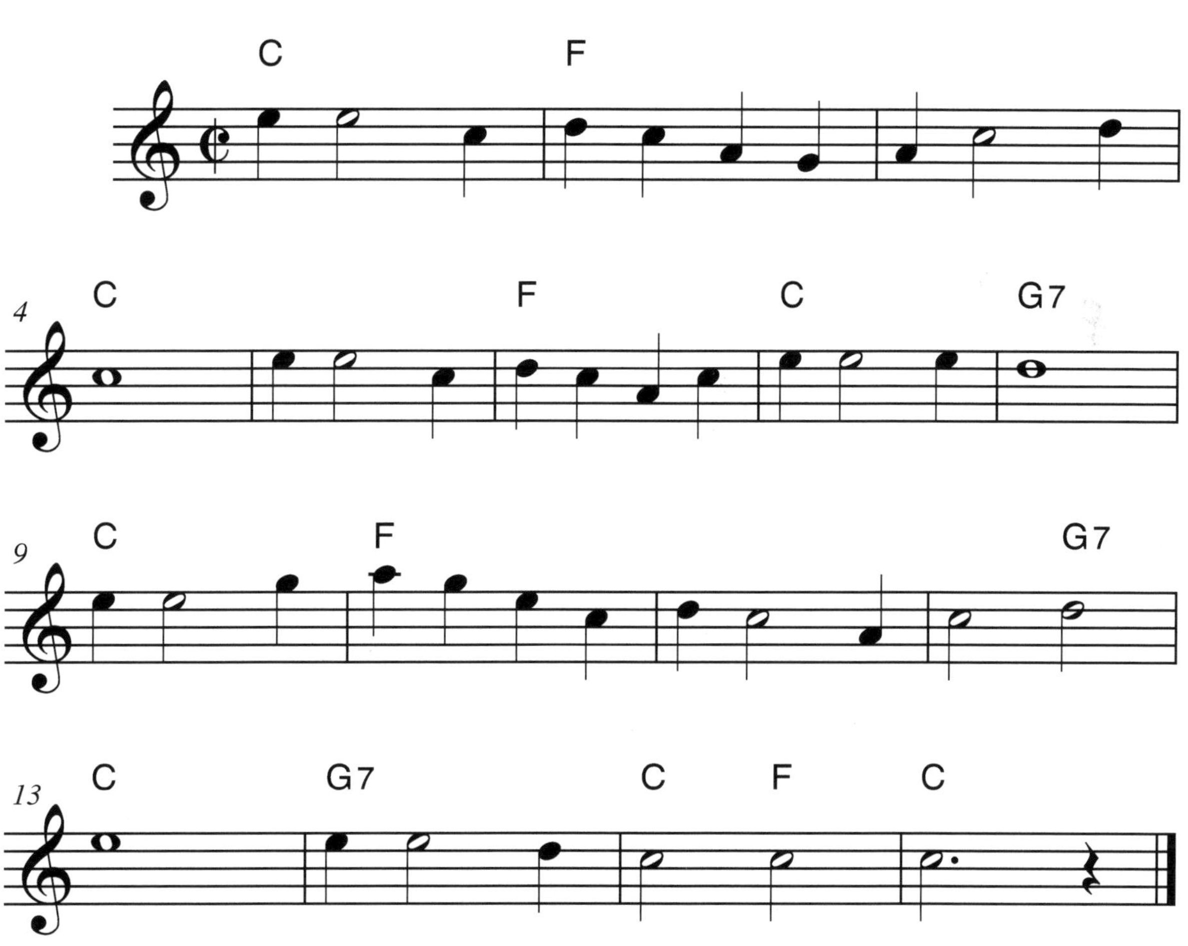

Goin' South

Oh, Sinner Man

Come & Go with Me to that Land

Bile' Dem Cabbage Down

Goober Peas

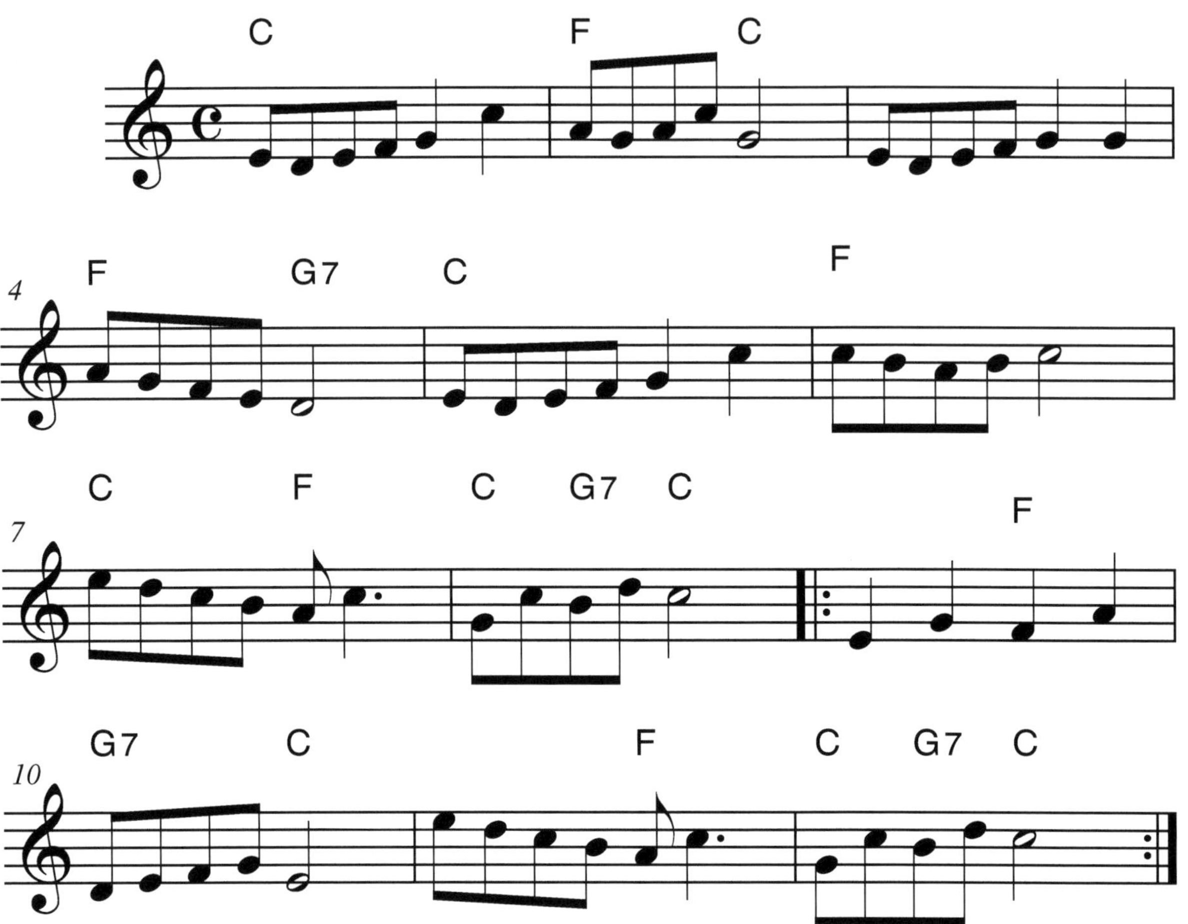

Captain Kidd

The Fish of the Sea

Jolly Old Roger

My Bonnie

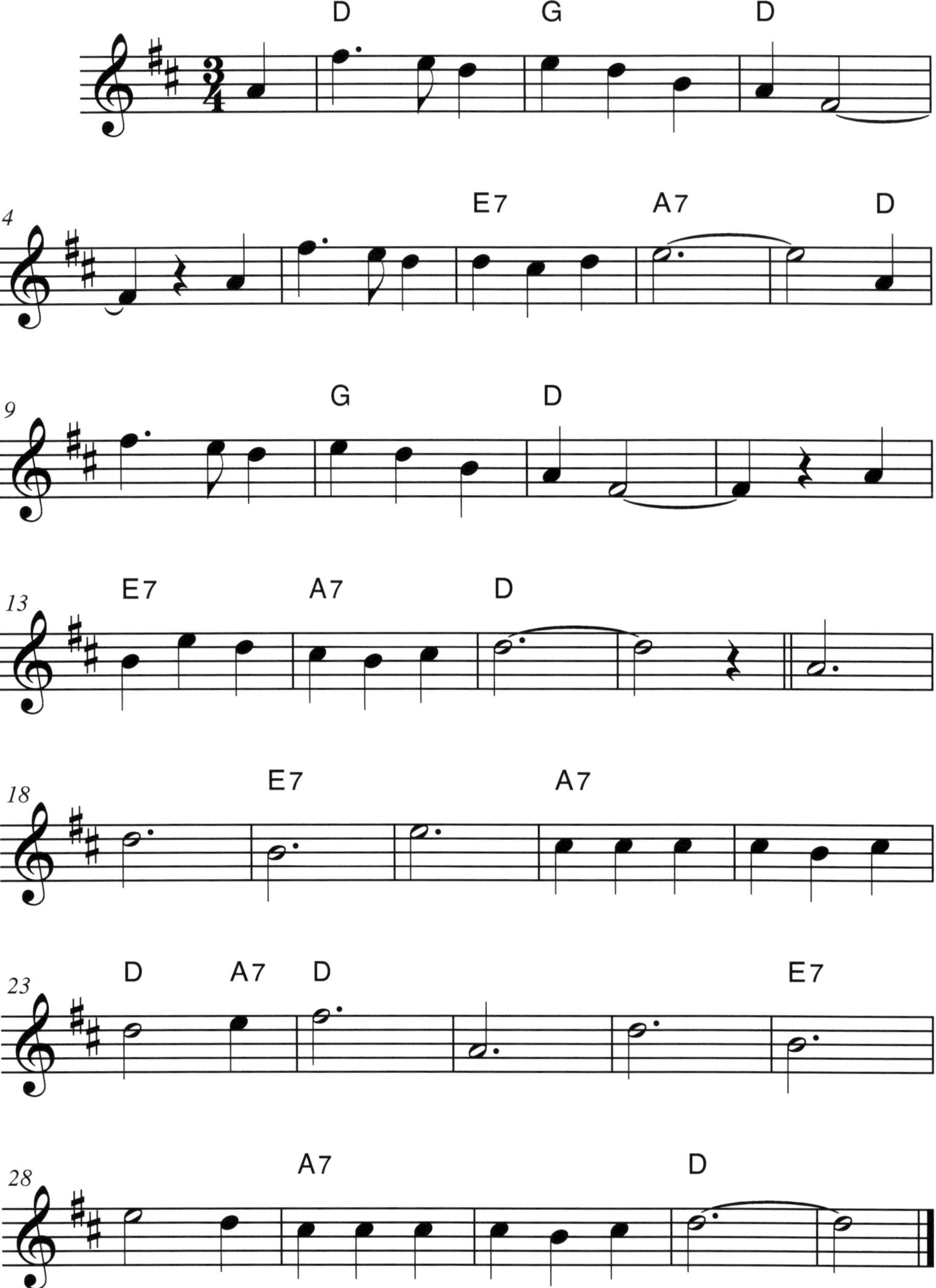
D   G   D
E7   A7   D
G   D
E7   A7   D
E7   A7
D   A7   D   E7
A7   D

The Bold Fisherman

High Barbaree

Greenland Fishery

Blow, Ye Winds

Cripple Creek

Sourwood Mountain

Big Rock Candy Mountain

The Roving Cowboy

When Jesus Wept

Blessed Quietness

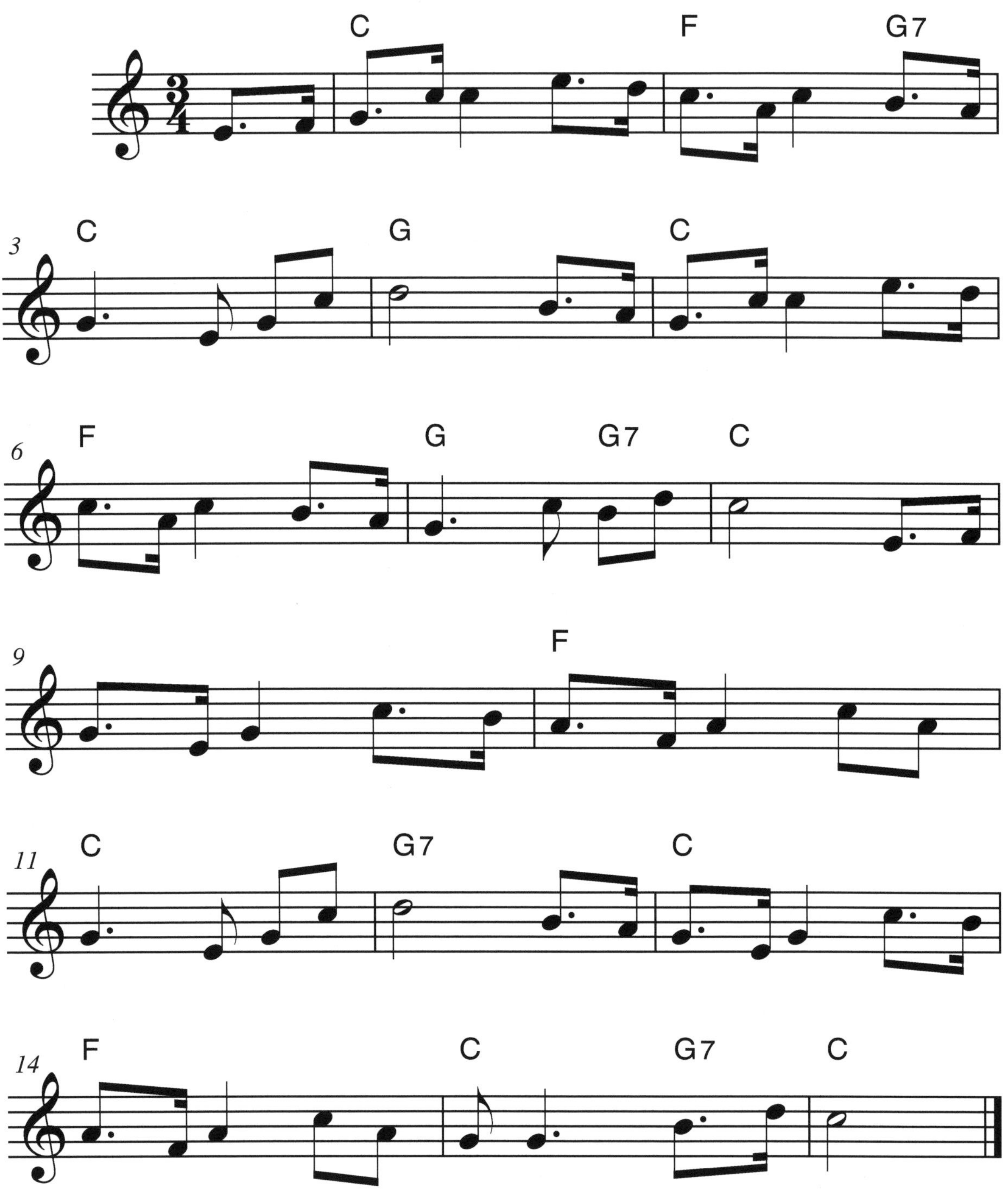

There's a River of Life

When I Can Read My Title Clear

Praise the Savior

Great God When I Approach Thy Throne

Early American

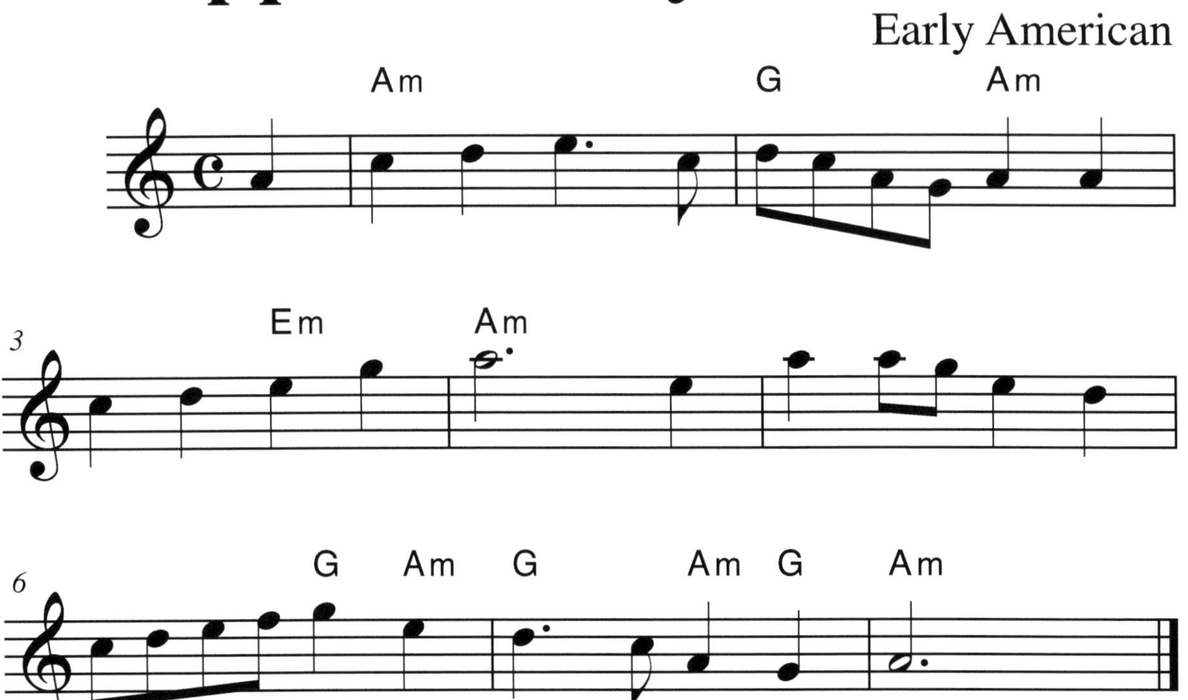

Must Jesus Bear The Cross Alone

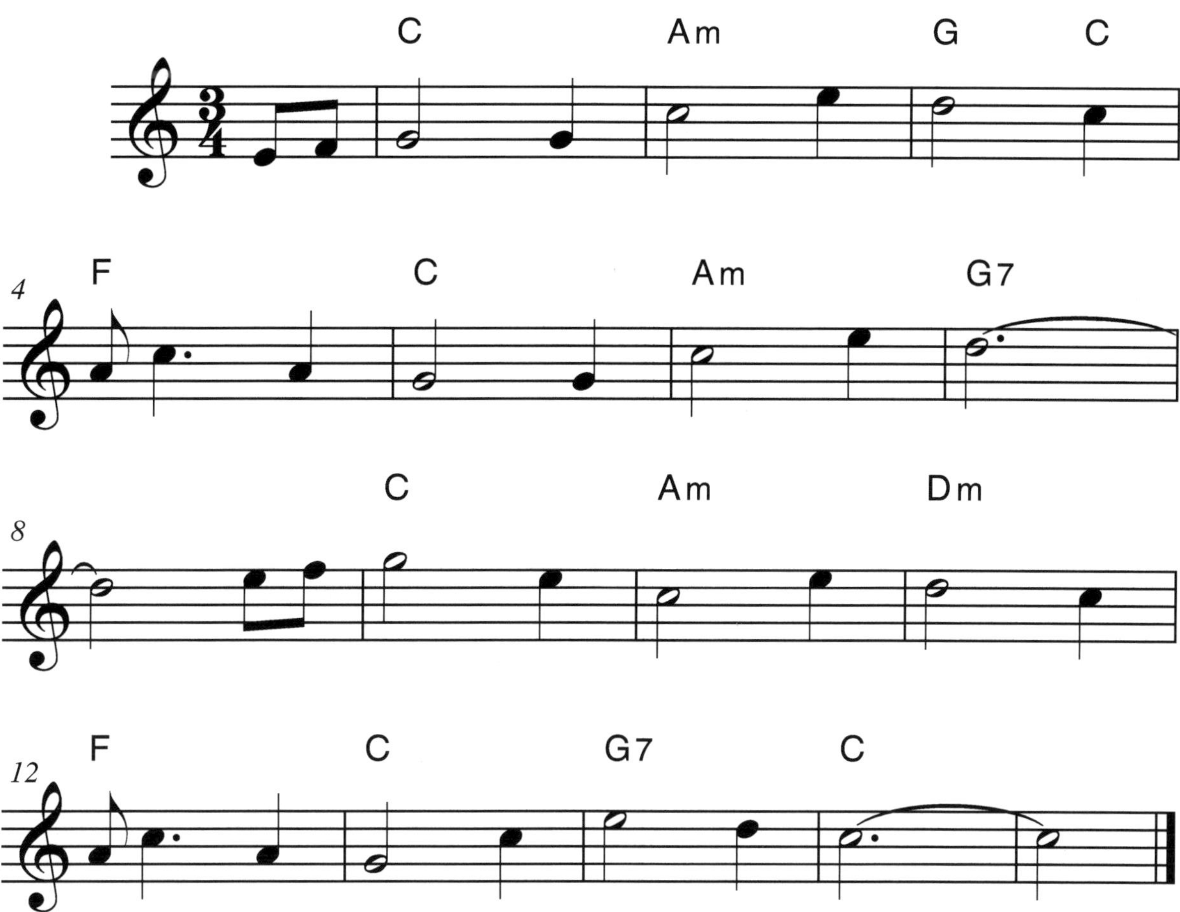

I am Bound for the Promised Land

When Jesus Left His Father's Throne

Jesus Calls Us

Lonesome Valley

The Galway Races

Cockles & Mussels

The Wild Rover

Love is Teasin'

The Galway Shawl

The Rose of Tralee

Brian O'linn

Spancil Hill

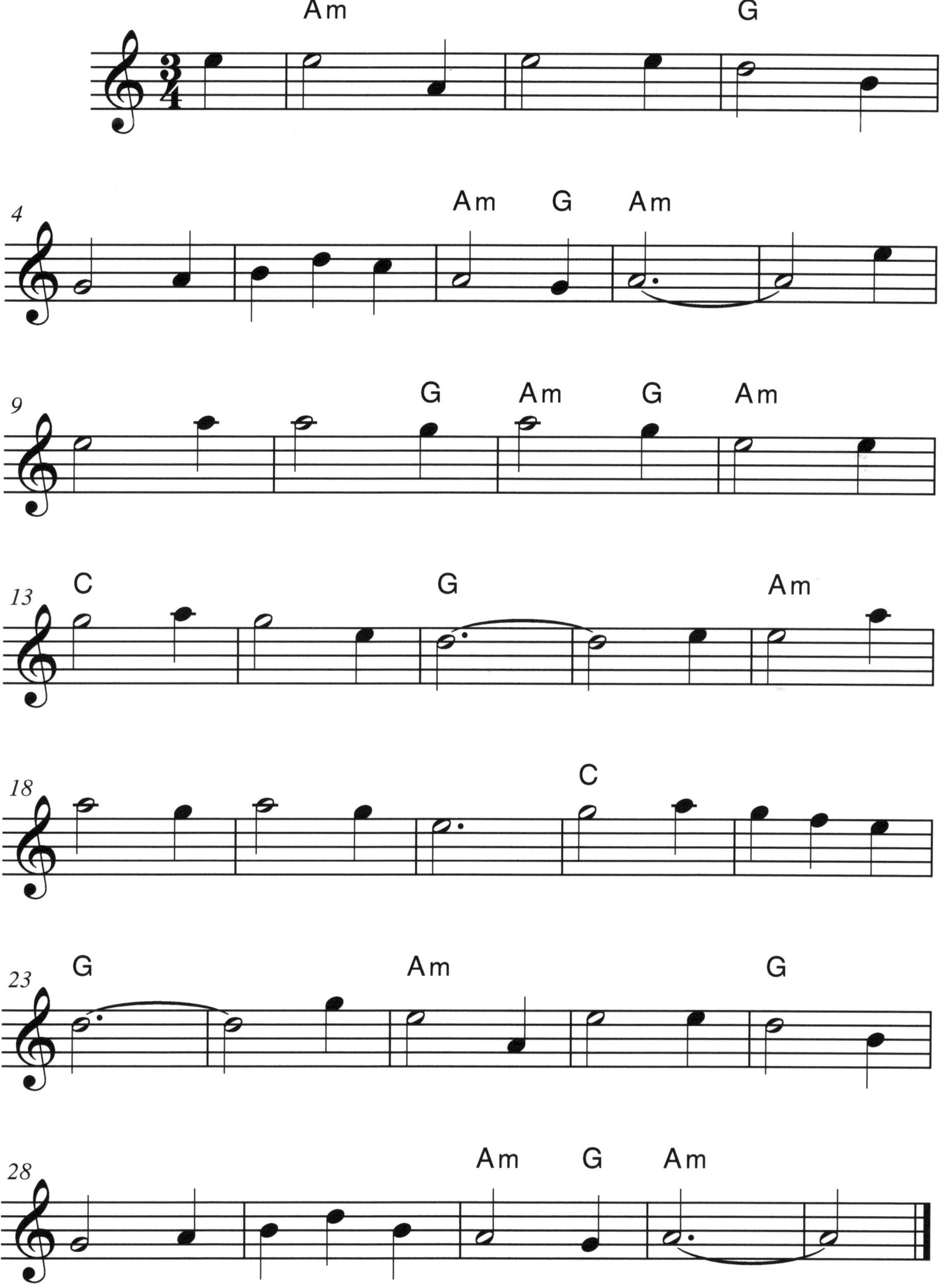

Si Beag Si Mór

Bunclody

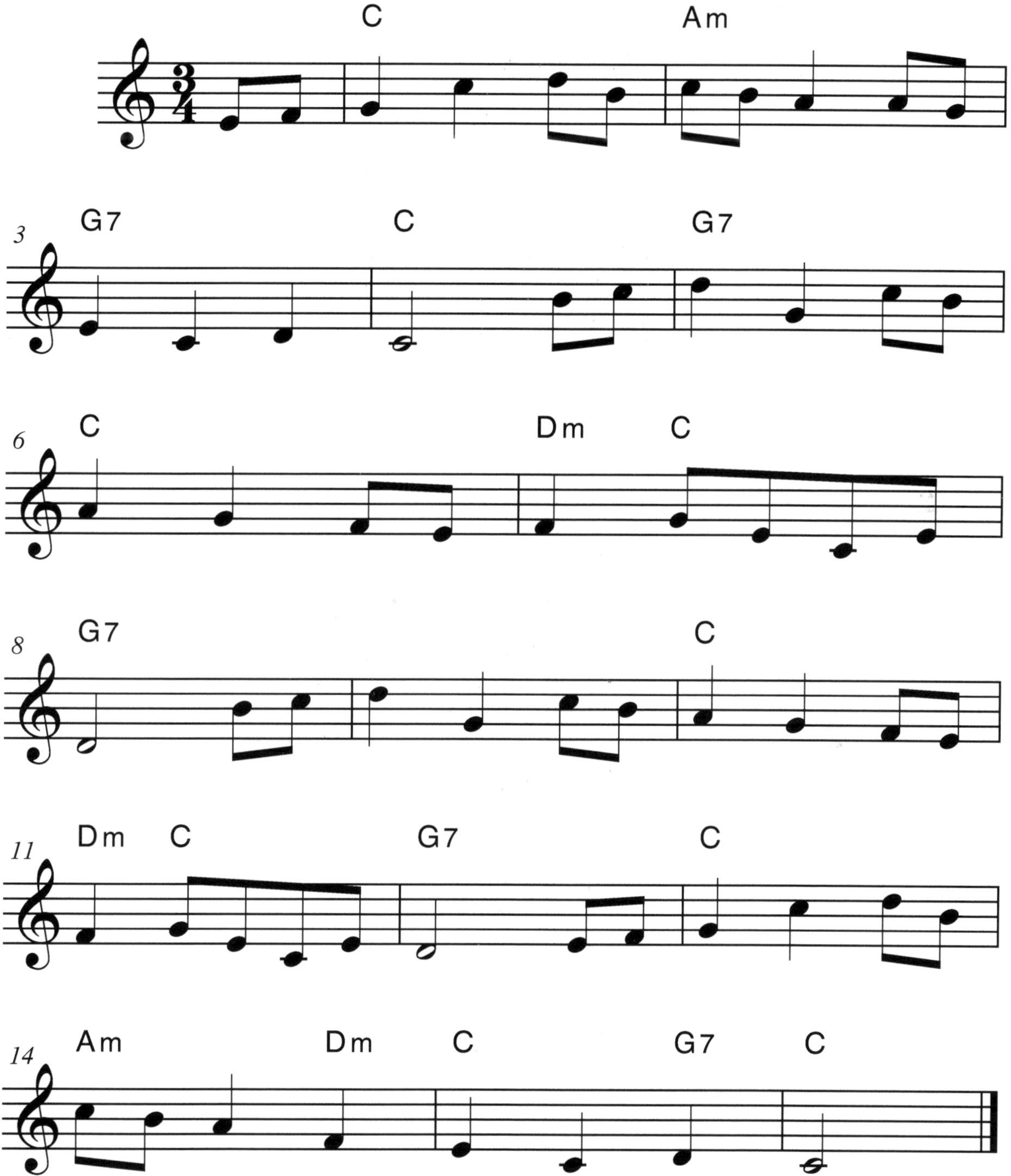

My Mary of the Curling Hair

Musetta's Waltz

Drink to Me Only with Thine Eyes

Southern Roses

Strauss

Gypsy Theme

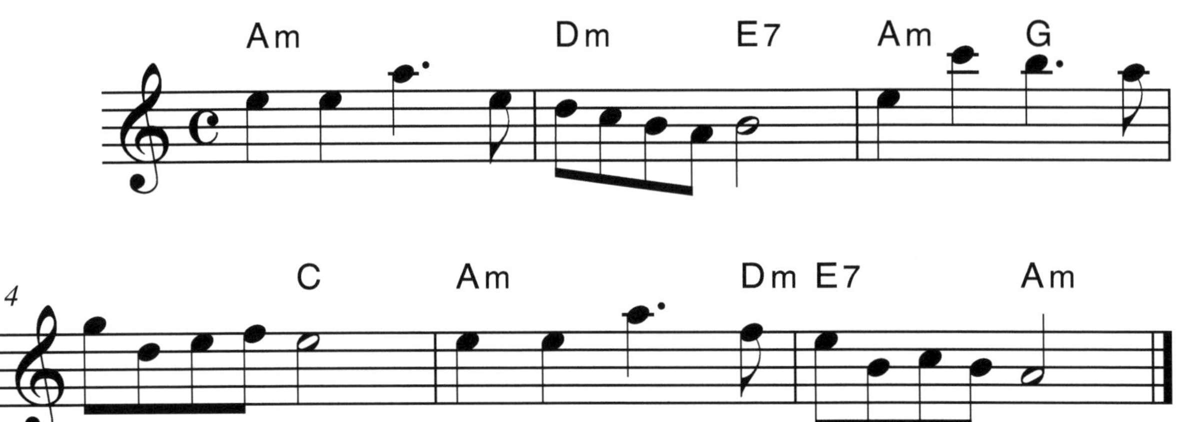

Am
Dm
E7
Am
G
C
Am
Dm E7
Am

Hatikvoh

Santa Lucia

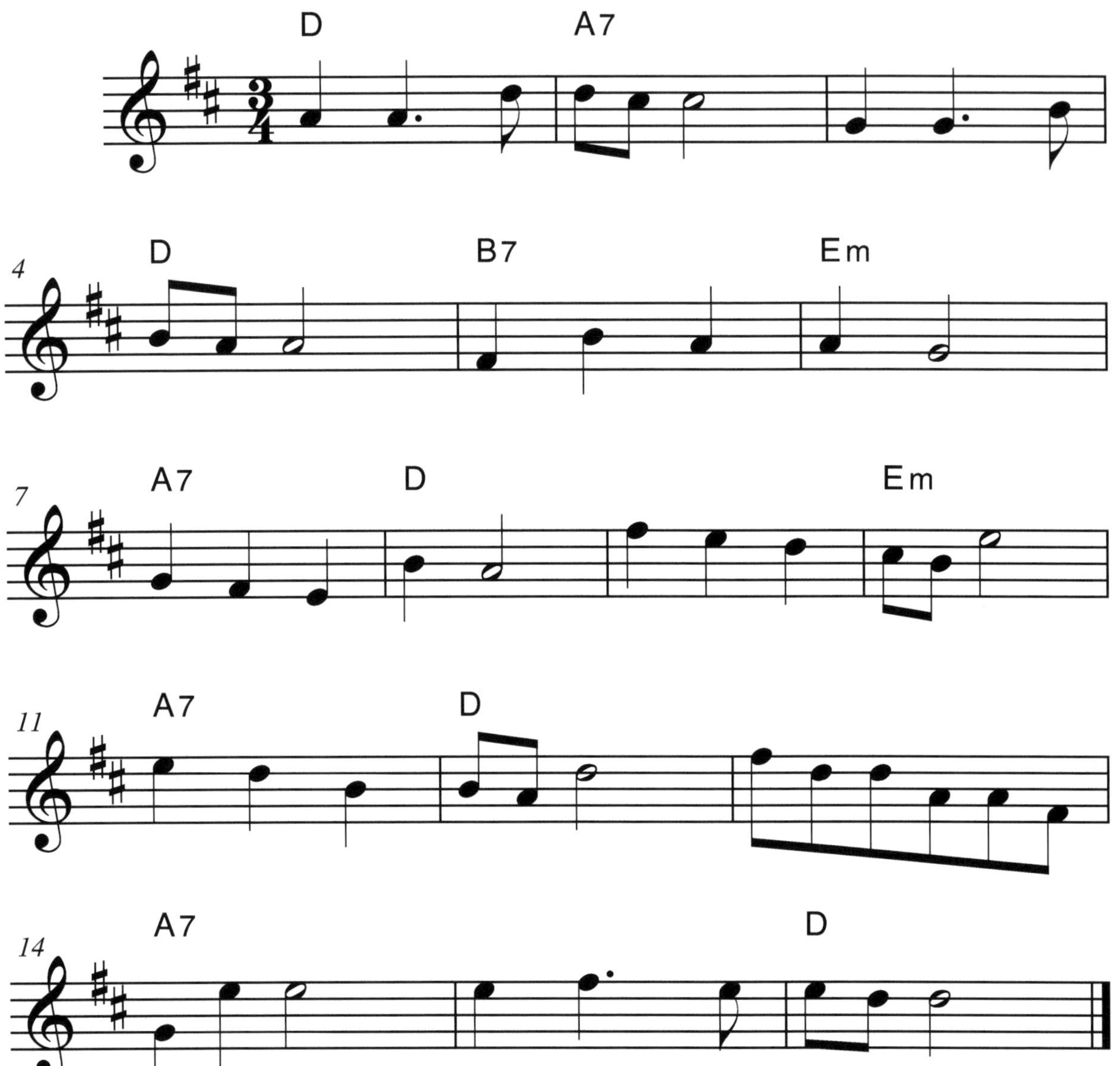
D
A7
D
B7
Em
A7
D
Em
A7
D
A7
D

Tis So Sweet

Gospel Song

68 I Need Thee Every Hour
Gospel Song
C   G7   C
F   C   G
C   G7
C   F   C   G
G7   C   F
C   G7   C   G7   C

Precious Memories

Gospel Song

Mandy Lee

American Ballad

Daisy Bell

Up in a Balloon

Strike Up the Band

74 This Little Light of Mine

Silver Threads Among the Gold

Grandfather's Clock

All God's Children Got Shoes

Little David Play on Your Harp

Spiritual

If You're Happy and You Know it

I've Got Peace Like a River

Bringing in the Sheaves

In the Pines

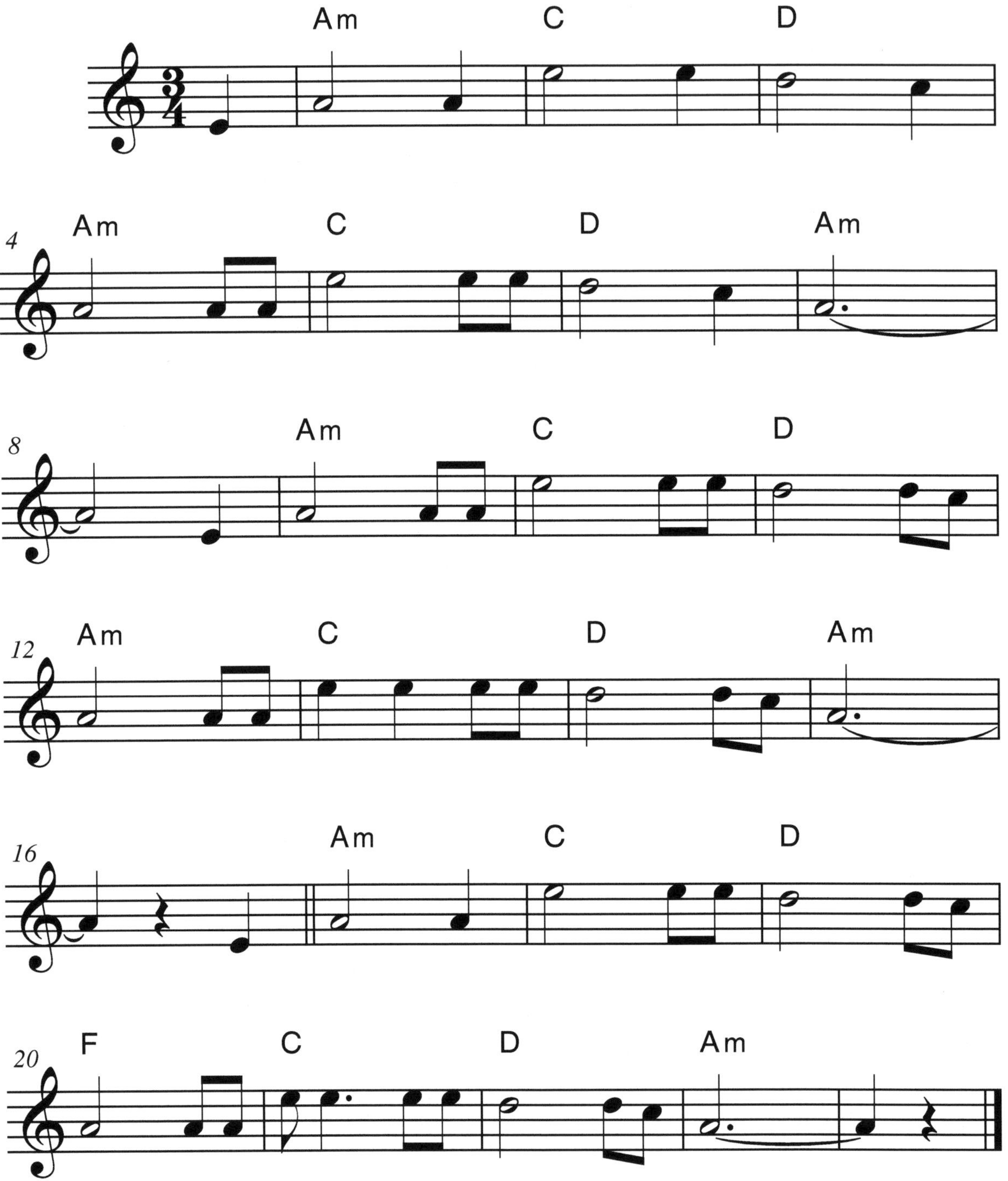

Am
C
D
Am
C
D
Am
Am
C
D
Am
C
D
Am
Am
C
D
F
C
D
Am

The Battle Cry of Freedom

Nine Hundred Miles

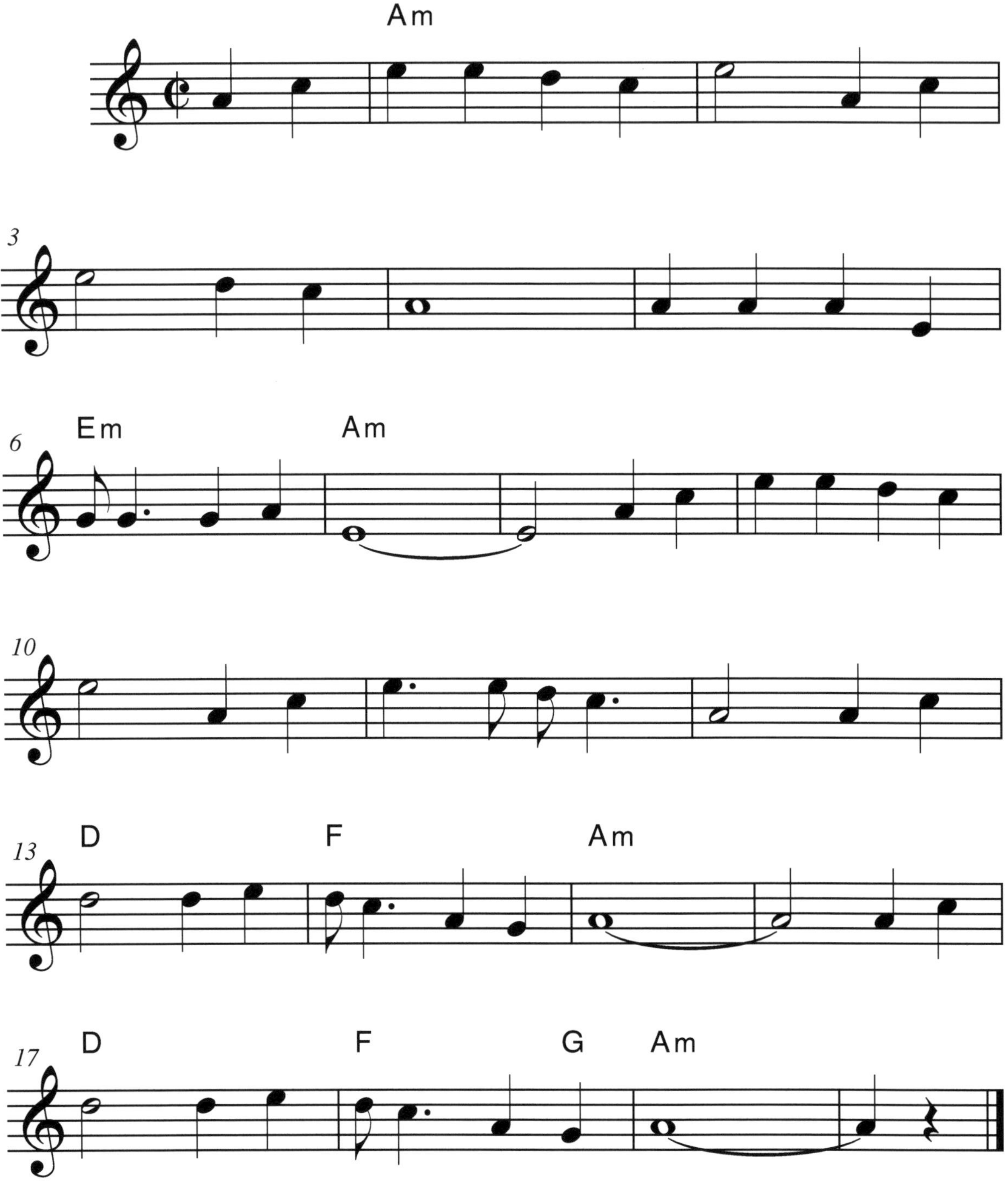

Down Where the Cotton Blossoms Grow

Lively Tempo

American Song

America the Beautiful

Our Boys will Shine Tonight

Columbia, the Gem of the Ocean

21
C
F
Dm
G7
C
23

Mama Don't 'Low

She'll Be Comin' Round the Mountain

Loch Lomond

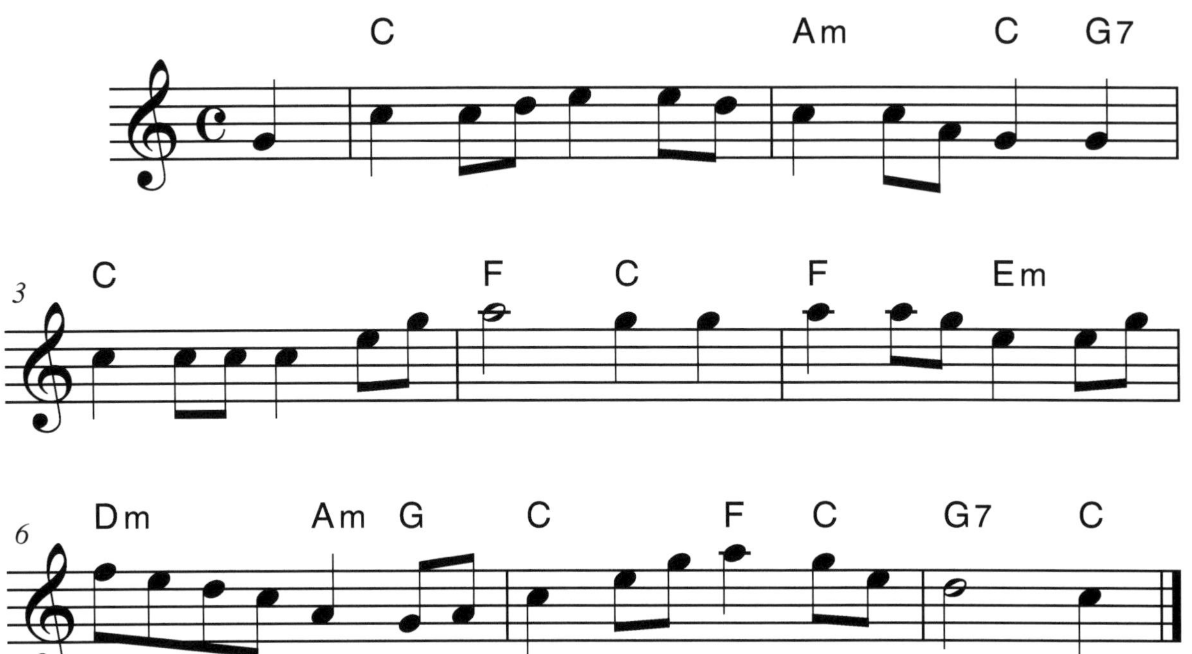

C   Am   C   G7
C   F   C   F   Em
Dm   Am   G   C   F   C   G7   C

Crawdad Song

The Mermaid

American Sailing Song

The Old Oaken Bucket

Doxology

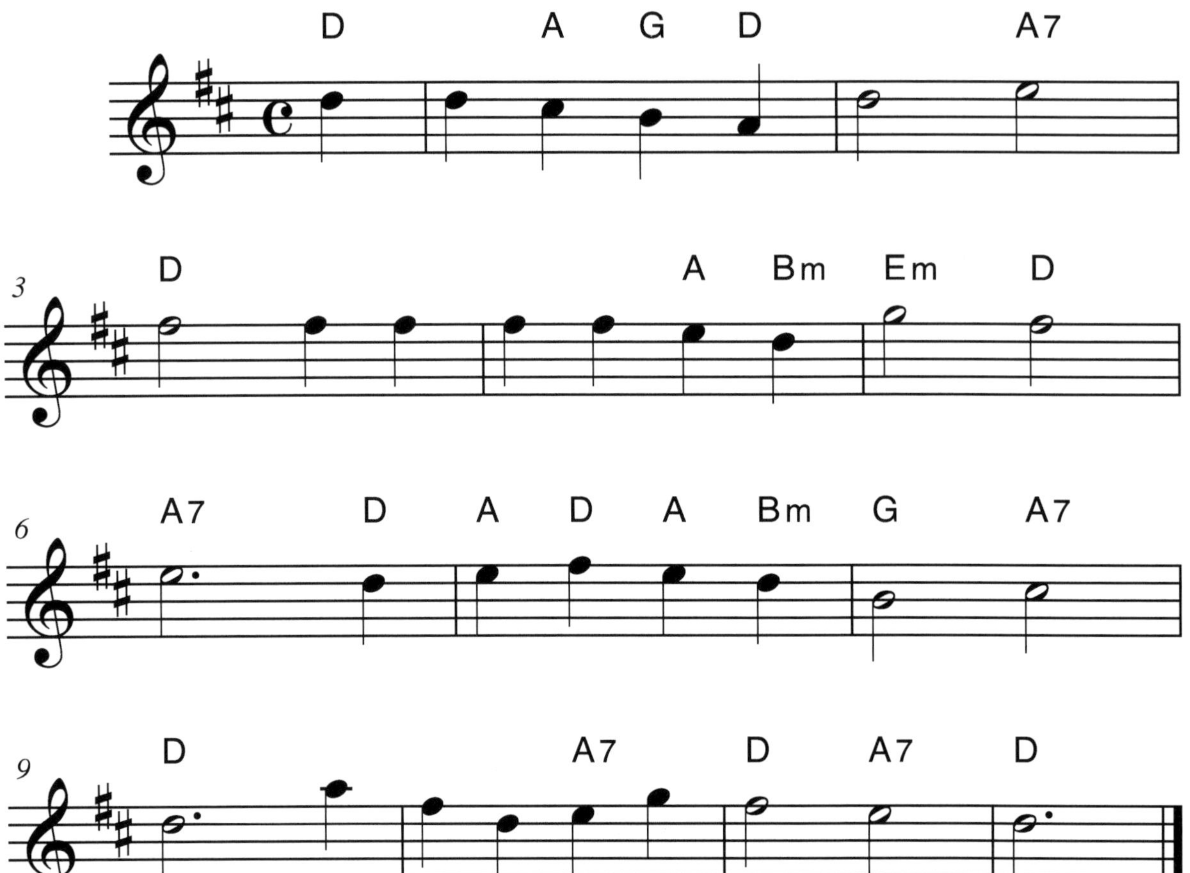

D   A G D   A7
D   A Bm Em D
A7   D   A D A Bm G   A7
D   A7   D A7   D

Made in the USA
Charleston, SC
16 February 2010